PIANO ACCOMPANIMENT
CHRISTMAS FAVORITES

Solos and String Orchestra Arrangements
Correlated with Essential Elements String Method

Arranged by
LLOYD CONLEY

Welcome to Essential Elements Christmas Favorites! There are two versions of each holiday selection in this versatile book. The SOLO version (with lyrics) appears in the beginning of each student book. The STRING ORCHESTRA arrangements of each song follows. The supplemental recording (CD or Cassette) or string orchestra PIANO PART may be used as an accompaniment for solo performance. The recording may also be used as a teaching aid in string orchestra rehearsals. The optional PERCUSSION book may be used with the FULL STRING ORCHESTRA arrangements. Create endless holiday programming possibilities with the accompaniment backgrounds and any combination of instruments!

ISBN 0-7935-8395-0

HAL•LEONARD®
CORPORATION
7777 W. BLUEMOUND RD. P.O. BOX 13819 MILWAUKEE, WI 53213

00868015

JINGLE BELLS

PIANO ACCOMPANIMENT

Words and Music by J. PIERPONT
Arranged by LLOYD CONLEY

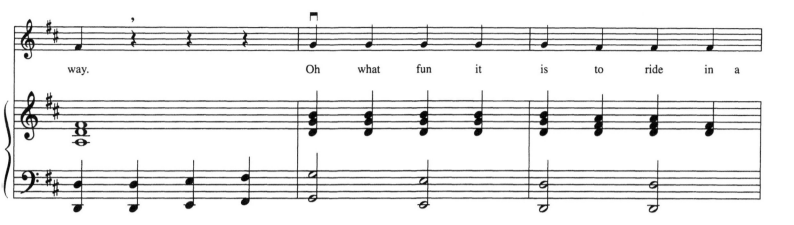

way. Oh what fun it is to ride in a

21

one horse o - pen sleigh!

Oh what fun it is to ride in a

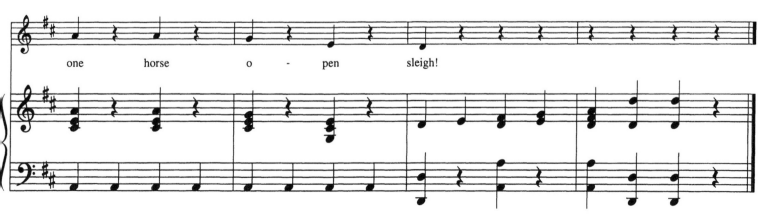

one horse o - pen sleigh!

UP ON THE HOUSETOP

PIANO ACCOMPANIMENT

Words and Music by B.R. HANDY
Arranged by LLOYD CONLEY

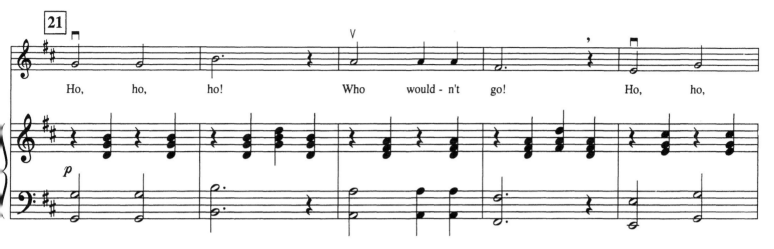

Ho, ho, ho! Who would-n't go! Ho, ho,

ho! Who would-n't go! Up on the house - top,

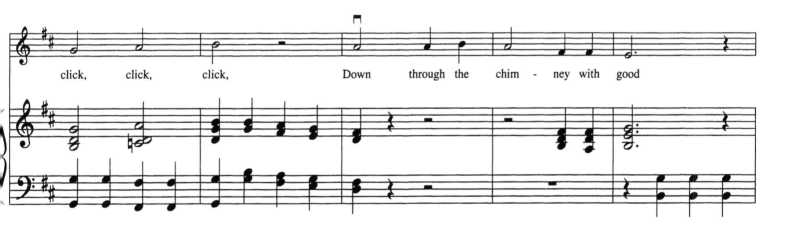

click, click, click, Down through the chim - ney with good

Saint Nick.

T E ANH AB S NG

PIANO ACCOMPANIMENT

Traditional
Arranged by LLOYD CONLEY

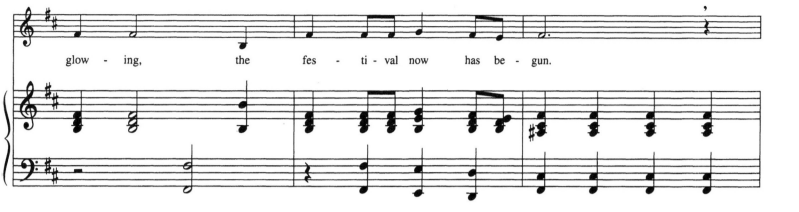

glow - ing, the fes - ti - val now has be - gun.

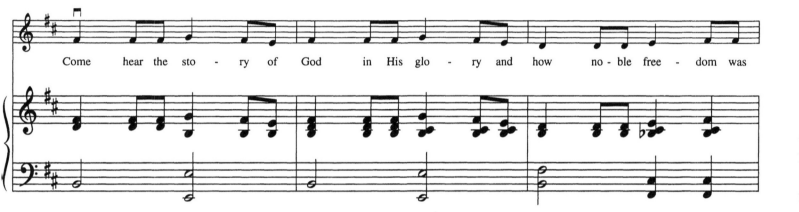

Come hear the sto - ry of God in His glo - ry and how no - ble free - dom was

won. Ha - nuk - kah, O Ha - nuk - kah, our voic - es are ring - ing.

21

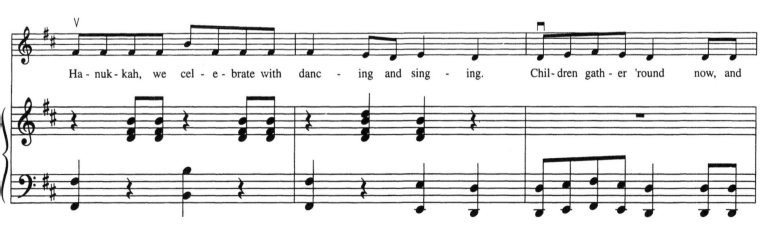

Ha - nuk - kah, we cel - e - brate with danc - ing and sing - ing. Chil - dren gath - er 'round now, and

light up the lights. Mir - a - cles of old are with - in us to-night. The can - dles are

glow - ing, the fes - ti - val now has be - gun. Come hear the sto - ry of

God in His glo - ry and now no - ble free - dom was won.

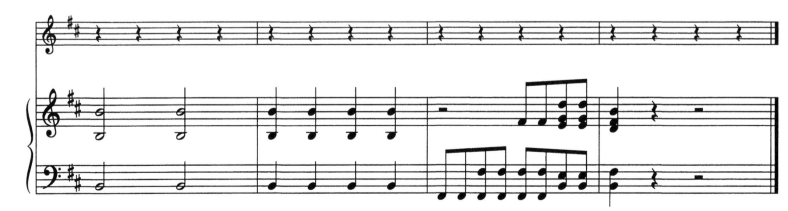

PIANO ACCOMPANIMENT

Traditional English Folksong
Arranged by LLOYD CONLEY

A Holly Jolly Christmas

PIANO ACCOMPANIMENT

Music and Lyrics by JOHNNY MARKS
Arranged by LLOYD CONLEY

00868015

12

Some - bod - y waits for you. Kiss her once for me. Have a hol - ly jol - ly

Christ - mas, and in case you did - n't hear, Oh, by gol - ly have a

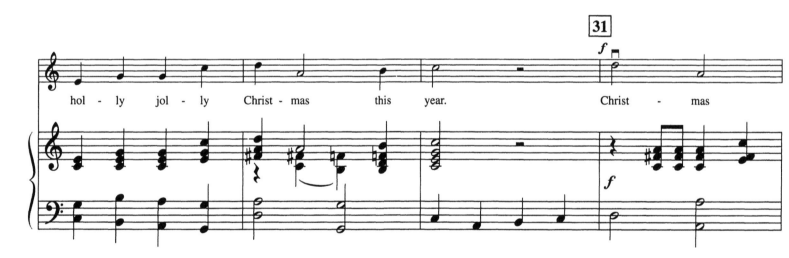

hol - ly jol - ly Christ - mas this year. Christ - mas

time this year.

FROSTY THE SNOW MAN

PIANO ACCOMPANIMENT

Words and Music by
STEVE NELSON and JACK ROLLINS
Arranged by LLOYD CONLEY

Lively (♩ = 112)

Fros - ty the snow man was a jol - ly hap - py soul,
Fros - ty the snow man is a fair - y tale they say,

With a corn cob pipe and a but - ton nose and two eyes made out of coal.
He was made of snow, but the chil - dren know how he came to life one day.

There

00868015

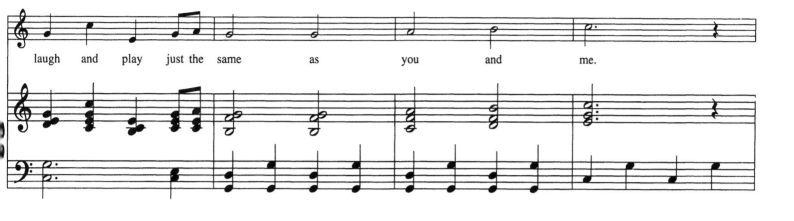

laugh and play just the same as you and me.

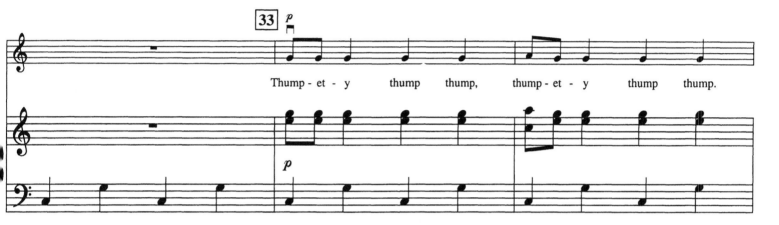

33 *p*

Thump - et - y thump thump, thump - et - y thump thump.

p

Look at Frost - y go. Thump - et - y thump thump,

thump - et - y thump thump. O - ver the hills of snow.

ROCKIN' AROUND THE CHRISTMAS TREE

PIANO ACCOMPANIMENT

Music and Lyrics by JOHNNY MARKS
Arranged by LLOYD CONLEY

Lat - er we'll have some pump - kin pie___ and we'll do some car - ol - ing.

21

You will get a sen - ti - men - tal feel - ing when you hear

voic - es sing - ing, "Let's be jol - ly, Deck the halls with boughs of hol - ly."

1.
Rock- in' a - round the Christ - mas tree.___ Have a hap - py hol - i - day.

Ev - 'ry - one danc - ing mer - ri - ly___ in the new old fash - ioned way.

2.

Rock - in' a - round the Christ - mas tree.___ Have a hap - py hol - i - day.

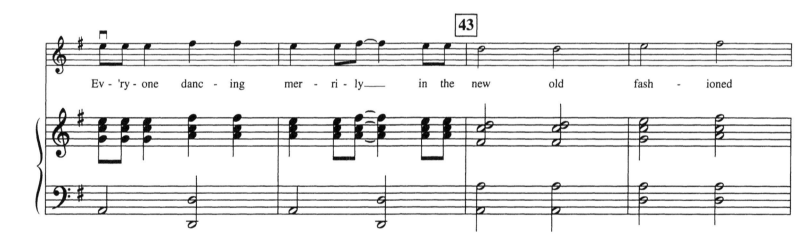

43

Ev - 'ry - one danc - ing mer - ri - ly___ in the new old fash - ioned

way.

JINGLE BELL ROCK

PIANO ACCOMPANIMENT

Words and Music by
JOE BEAL and JIM BOOTHE
Arranged by LLOYD CONLEY

bright time, it's the right time to rock the night a - way. Jin - gle -

bell time is a swell time to go glid - in' in a one - horse sleigh.

Gid - dy - ap, jin - gle - horse pick up your feet. Jin - gle a - round the clock.

Mix and min - gle in a jin - gle - in' beat. That's the jin - gle - bell

SILVER BELLS
From the Paramount Picture THE LEMON DROP KID

Words and Music by
JAY LIVINGSTON and RAY EVANS
Arranged by LLOYD CONLEY

PIANO ACCOMPANIMENT

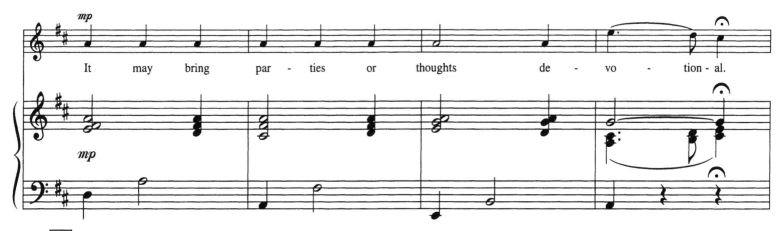

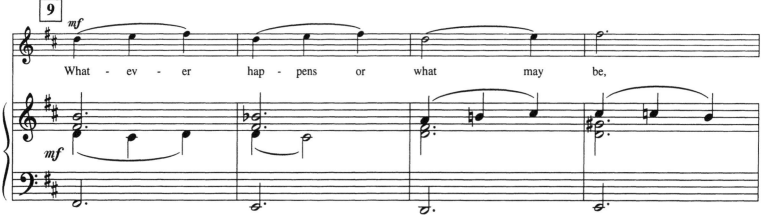

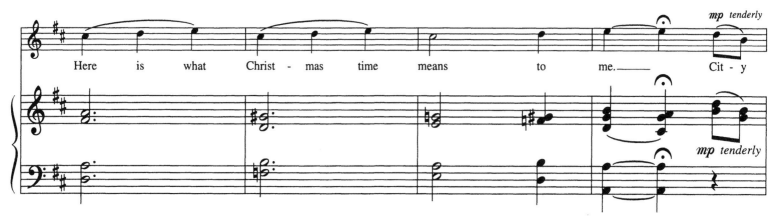

00868015

It's Christ - mas time in the cit - y.

36

Ring - a - ling, hear them ring,

Soon it will be Christ - mas day.

rit.

Let It Snow! Let It Snow!
Let It Snow!

PIANO ACCOMPANIMENT

Words by SAMMY CAHN
Music by JULE STYNE
Arranged by LLOYD CONLEY

13

doesn't show signs of stop-ing, And I brought some corn for pop-ping, The

lights are turned way down low, Let it snow! Let it snow! Let it snow! When we

21

fi-nal-ly kiss good-night, How I'll hate go-ing out in the storm! But if

you'll real-ly hold me tight All the way home I'll be warm. The

fire is slow - ly dy - ing And my dear we're still good-bye - ing, But as

long as you love me so, Let it snow! Let it snow! Let it snow! When we

snow!

Faster (♩ = 132)

WHITE CHRISTMAS
From the Motion Picture Irving Berlin's HOLIDAY INN

Words and Music by
IRVING BERLIN
Arranged by LLOYD CONLEY

PIANO ACCOMPANIMENT

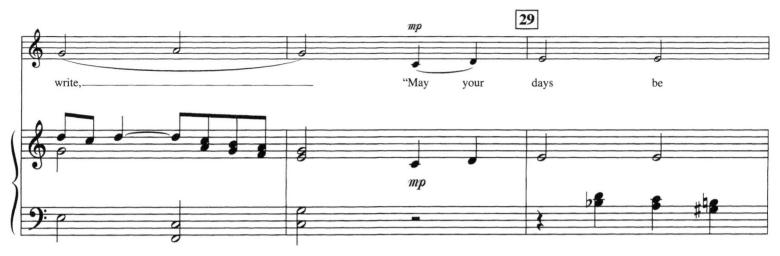

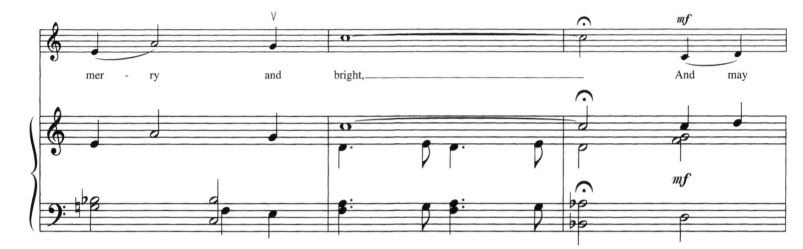

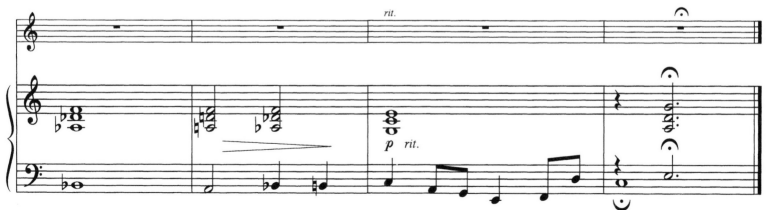